HOW IT WAS
BRITAIN AT WAR 1914-18

Stewart Ross

Daddy, what did _YOU_ do in the Great War?

B. T. Batsford Ltd, London

© Stewart Ross 1993

First published 1993

Typeset by Goodfellow & Egan, Ltd, Cambridge and printed in Hong Kong

Published by
B. T. Batsford Ltd
4 Fitzhardinge Street
London W1H 0AH

A CIP catalogue record for this book is available from the British Library.

ISBN 0 7134 7260 X

Frontispiece: *A famous World War I recruitment poster. It was intended to make men who did not volunteer feel guilty.*

Introduction illustration: *Still from film of the Battle of the Somme, 1916.*

Cover illustration: Over the Top *by John Nash.*

INTRODUCTION

When Britain went to war with Germany at midnight on 4 August 1914, the country had not fought a full-scale war for nearly a century. The industrial revolution and the wealth from an enormous overseas empire had enabled Britain to prosper as never before. The Royal Navy, far larger than any other maritime fighting force, had guarded British shores and protected worldwide trade routes. A small army, based largely in the colonies, had been sufficient to take care of most military needs. Proud of their achievements and supremely confident, many British believed they were the most powerful nation on earth. The war would be 'over by Christmas', they declared. And they would be victorious.

In fact, by Christmas 1914 the war had hardly begun. It dragged on for almost another four years, spreading right round the globe, taking millions of lives, costing an untold fortune, overthrowing age-old dynasties and redrawing the political map of the world. In the end, Britain survived with its empire intact and could number itself among the victorious. But British society had been shaken to its foundations, and the country's economic and industrial strength severely battered: its boast of world supremacy lay among the corpses of the battlefield.

By 1915 it was clear that the 'Great War', as it was already being called, was quite unlike any other the world had experienced. It involved more people, not just soldiers at the front, but those at home who had to endure unprecedented hardships and change. Survival depended on the efforts of the whole nation: farmers, factory workers, shopkeepers and bankers, as well as soldiers, sailors and airmen. Moreover, it was a technological war. Individual acts of bravery, even daring strategic ploys, were useless without sufficient hardware to back them up. It was the war of the submarine and torpedo, the machine gun and tank, barbed wire, aeroplanes, telephones, poison gas and mortars. Above all, it was a war of grinding attrition. For most of the conflict, the weapons of defence and blockade were superior to those of attack. Victory, when it eventually came, was brought by no dashing triumph in a single battle. It resulted from wearing down the enemy, at home as well as in the field, until eventually they lost the will to continue

the senseless struggle. This book explains Britain's part in the Great War: the way the armed forces were raised and equipped, life at home, the peace settlement and the terrible battles fought on land, sea and in the air for four long, gruelling years.

Introductory quiz

Do you know?
What *Blighty* was?

Why soldiers in the trenches placed buckets of water in the ground?

How many men were called up into the British army in the First World War?

Who were Britain's war allies?

Why convoys were first used?

How long a British front line pilot could expect to live in the spring of 1917?

The First World War began as a European war, the terrible and unforseen consequence of rivalries which had divided the major powers of the continent for decades.

The origins of conflict may be traced back to the startling events of 1870–1. In 1870, Prussia (the most powerful of the German states) and its German allies went to war with France, which was soon defeated. In January 1871 the victors came together to form the German Empire, and at the peace treaty in May the new empire gained the French provinces of Alsace and Lorraine. These dramatic moves upset the balance of power in Europe. They also left France and Germany, now the major military and industrial force on the Continent, implacable enemies.

Fearing a French revenge attack, the German chancellor Bismarck used diplomacy to keep his enemy isolated. He arranged a defensive Dual Alliance with Austria-Hungary (1879), joined by Italy in 1882, and a special agreement with Russia. With the accession of Emperor (*Kaiser*) William II in 1888, however, Bismarck fell from favour and France was able to end her isolation. Shortly after the chancellor's resignation in 1890, France and Russia formed an alliance, which threatened Germany on both her western and eastern frontiers.

The European countries involved in the First World War. The Allies are coloured pink, Germany and her allies yellow, and neutral countries green. Except for Russia, which left the war in 1917, the dates in brackets refer to the years in which countries entered the war. Where no year is given, the date is 1914.

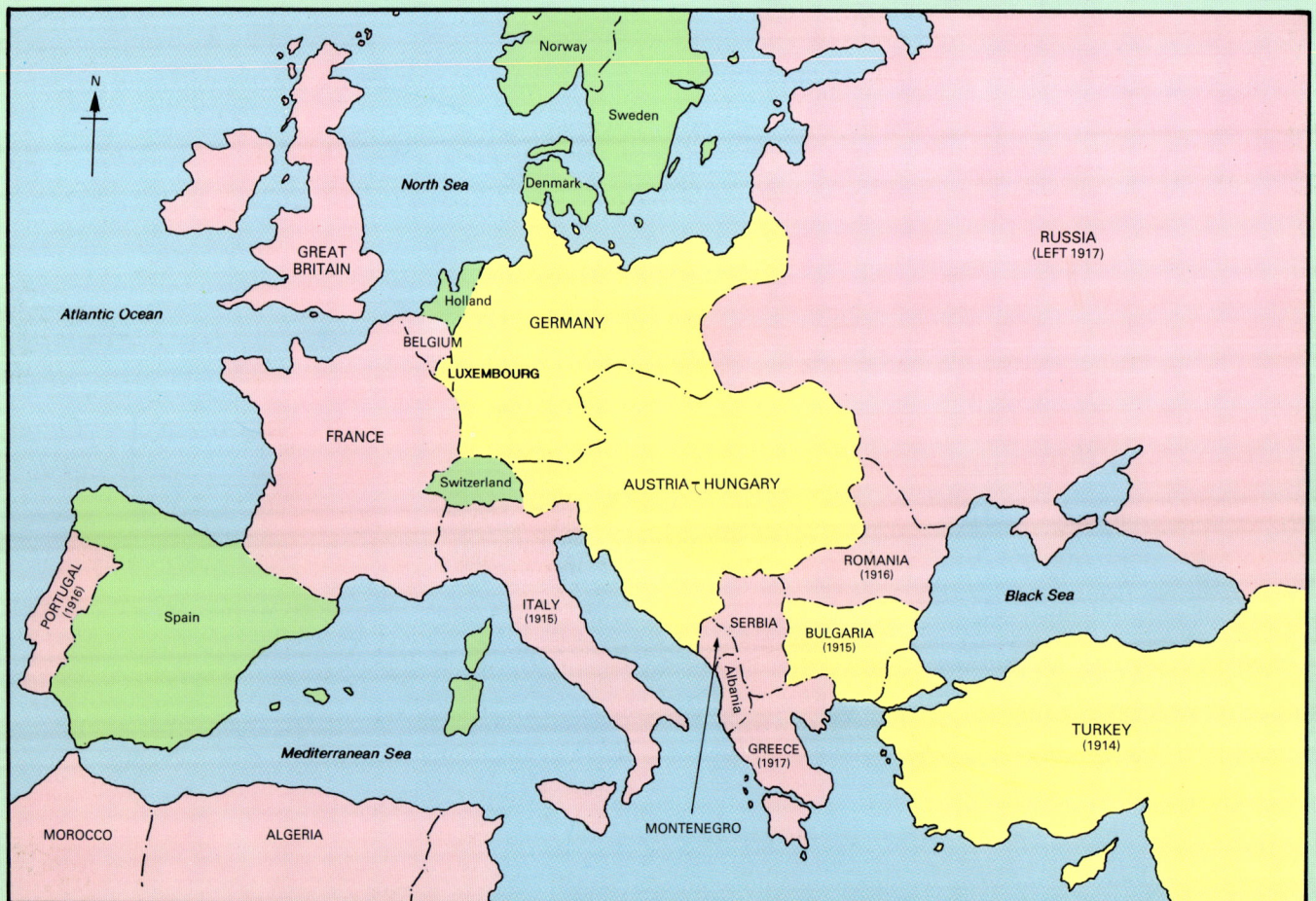

Hitherto, Britain had regarded Germany quite favourably. British governments were more concerned with overseas colonies than Europe; they saw French ambitions as the greatest threat to the British empire. But towards the end of the century, as Germany built up a large navy and joined in the scramble for colonies, particularly in Africa, and with British businesses meeting fierce German competition in world markets, Anglo-German relations began to deteriorate. Each power blamed the other for what was happening.

Until 1902, when it signed a treaty with Japan, Britain had believed itself strong enough to survive outside the network of alliances. But the government felt increasingly vulnerable, and in 1904 it came to an *entente* (understanding) with France. An Anglo-Russian entente followed in 1907. This divided Europe into two armed camps: the Triple Alliance of Germany, Austria and, less committedly, Italy, confronting the Triple Entente of France, Russia and Britain. Both sides engaged in a dangerous arms race, building up their forces to get ahead of their enemies. As the armies and navies of the Triple Entente were potentially much stronger than those of the Triple Alliance, the

German High Command argued that if ever war seemed inevitable, they ought to strike first. To this end, they devised a strategy – the Schlieffen Plan – to sweep into France from the north-west and put the old enemy swiftly out of action.

In June 1914 Archduke Franz Ferdinand, heir to the Austrian throne, was assassinated in the Balkan town of Sarajevo. Backed by Germany, the Austrians blamed Russia's ally Serbia and attacked the country on 28 July. Four days later Russia was at war with Germany. Fearing an attack in the west, Germany declared war on Russia's ally France (3 August), and put the Schlieffen Plan into operation. German troops moved into Belgium, whose neutrality Britain had guaranteed. The Kaiser refused to withdraw his forces, and on the morning of 5 August the British people awoke to find themselves at war.

Le Petit Journal: A French cartoon of 1914 showing the German Kaiser watching his forces attack Arras. The subtitle reads: 'The barbarian contemplates his work.' Why are the picture and the caption likely to be propaganda?

THE DRIFT TO WAR

Historians speak of long-term and short-term causes of the First World War. The long-term causes, such as European nationalism, the division of the continent into two armed camps, the arms race, economic rivalry and the problems arising out of the decline of the Turkish Empire and the emergence of the German Empire, created an atmosphere in which war was possible. The short-term causes, including the assassination of Archduke Franz Ferdinand, Germany's decision to back Austria-Hungary against Serbia and Germany's use of the Schlieffen Plan, explain how this dangerous situation turned into war.

The Schlieffen Plan

Germany's plan to defeat France with a rapid encircling movement round Paris was devised by Count Alfred von Schlieffen, Chief of the German General Staff, 1891–1905. It was later adapted by his successor, Helmuth von Moltke, as shown in the diagram opposite. Faced with the possibility of an overwhelming attack from both France and Russia, the Germans felt they had no option but to strike first. Would it be accurate, therefore, to describe the Schlieffen Plan as a major short-term explanation for the outbreak of a Europe-wide conflict in 1914?

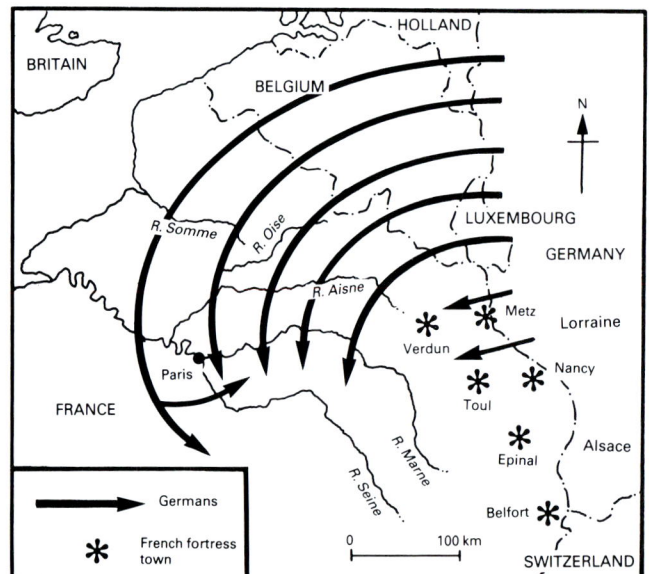

THINGS TO DO

1   List as many (a) long-term causes and (b) short-term causes of the World War as you can find.
2   Imagine you are a member of the Austro-Hungarian government in July 1914. Say what you hope to achieve by the ultimatum sent to Serbia.
3   Explain why it is probably unwise to blame any single country for the outbreak of the First World War.

CHECK YOUR UNDERSTANDING

Can you remember the meaning of the following words and phrase?

Entente
Neutral
Kaiser
Arms Race
Alliance
Ultimatum

(Top) *Cadets training in Cambridgeshire before the war, part of a growth in armed forces taking place across Europe.*

(Bottom) *The Schlieffen plan – why do you think the French concentrated their forces near Verdun, Metz, Nancy and Epinal?*

The Balkans

For hundreds of years the Balkans had been part of the empire of the Muslim Ottoman Turks. When this empire began to break up in the nineteenth century, the peoples of the region set up their own small nations, such as Serbia, Montenegro and Bulgaria. As well as being hostile to each other, these states were regarded with greedy eyes by the neighbouring empires of Austria-Hungary and Russia. In 1856, Britain and France had gone to war with Russia to prevent that country from expanding into the Balkans. After the assassination of Archduke Franz Ferdinand, Austria-Hungary sent Serbia a 10-point ultimatum. The Serbs had to accept all its points, or face invasion. Here are two of those points – why do you think the Serbs found them impossible to accept?

3. to eliminate . . . from public instruction everything that serves . . . the propaganda against Austria-Hungary, both where teachers and books are concerned.

4. to remove from military service and from the admin-istration all officers and officials who are guilty of having taken part in the propaganda against Austria-Hungary. [The Austro-Hungarians would provide a list of all those they wished removed.]

(Cited in I. Geiss, ed., *July 1914, Selected Documents*, 1967)

A 'Bolt From The Blue'

It has often been said that Britain stumbled into war in 1914. As the future prime minister Harold Macmillan remembered, it was a conflict few people predicted or wanted:

The First World War . . . burst like a bombshell upon ordinary people. It came suddenly and unexpectedly – a real 'bolt from the blue' . . . Indeed, in the summer of 1914, there was far more anxiety about civil war in Ireland than about a world war in Europe. Certainly, had we been told, when enjoying the carefree life of Oxford [University] in the summer term of 1914, that in a few weeks all of our little band of friends would abandon for ever academic life and rush to take up arms . . . we should have thought such prophesies the ravings of a maniac . . . Germany, after all, appeared to be governed by men of solid reputations and a civilised back-ground . . .

Even when war came, the general view was that it would be over by Christmas. Our major anxiety was by hook or by crook not to miss it.

(Harold Macmillan, *Winds of Change, 1914–1939*, 1966)

Q

With what justification do you think the Balkans were described as the 'powder keg of Europe'?

CAN YOU REMEMBER ?

Which provinces did Germany take from France in 1871?
Who was assassinated on 28 June 1914?
Which part of Europe was believed to be a 'powder keg'?
Why did Anglo-German relations deteriorate towards the end of the nineteenth century?
Name the countries of (a) the Triple Alliance and (b) the Triple Entente.

THE WESTERN FRONT

The Schlieffen Plan almost succeeded. The German armies came within sight of Paris but failed to break through the final few kilometres to the capital. In a battle fought around the River Marne in early September 1914, the French, aided by the small British Expeditionary Force, held the enemy advance long enough for reinforcements to arrive.

For the next few weeks both sides tried in vain to outflank each other. Each move extended the battlefront along a wider and wider line, until by October it snaked from the Belgian coast, south past Ypres to the River Somme, then roughly south-east to Verdun before twisting due south to Belfort and the Swiss border. The French held the greater part of the line, with the Belgians at the northern tip and the British concentrated in the two sectors between Ypres and Loos, and on either side of the River Somme.

The battlefields of France and Belgium (the Western Front) were clearly marked by rows of trenches and barbed wire and, in some places, by more substantial defences such as concrete bunkers. The reason for the front's lack of movement is clear from the nature of these defences – no matter how many they were, it was almost impossible for foot-soldiers to cross No Man's Land between opposing trenches and pierce the enemy line. And it was certainly not for want of trying.

The French made the first attempt to break the stalemate by attacking around Champagne during the winter and spring of 1914–15. By the middle of March they had advanced 8 kilometres at a cost of some 90,000 men. The first British attack followed immediately. Aimed at Lille, it took a kilometre of German territory for the loss of 13,000 men. Ghastly though the slaughter had been, it was one of the more effective offensives of the war. In May 27,000 were lost taking a kilometre of land near Artois. In the autumn more than twice that number fell in another attack in the same area. But this was nothing compared to the 419,000 casualties (58,000 on the first day) suffered during the Somme offensive by over half a million men between 1 July and 18 November 1916. The furthest advance was less than 10 kilometres.

Things were no better in 1917. British offensives at Arras (150,000 casualties) and in the mud around Ypres (310,000 casualties) gained little ground. The only notable successes were the undermining of an entire section of the German line near Messines and blowing it up with a million pounds of high

explosive (the sound carried clearly to London) and the first effective use of tanks near Cambrai. By Christmas that year each side on the Western front had suffered hundreds of thousands of casualties. Yet the lines of trenches remained virtually where they had been three years before.

'Oppy Wood 1917, *a painting by official British war artist Paul Nash, showing the desolate horror of the front line.*

THE WESTERN FRONT

It now seems extraordinary to us that the horrible slaughter of the Western Front should have gone on for so long without someone calling a halt. There were mutinies, notably among the French, and troops on both sides tried to get slight wounds so that they could be sent home – back to 'Blighty' the British called it. But attack after attack, year after year, the great majority of troops, politicians and civilians back home accepted what was happening as if there were no alternative.

Patriotism

Moved by a desire 'not to let the side down', men fought out of loyalty to their country and their company. The government seized on this sentiment, reinforcing it with clever propaganda. Lord Kitchener's recruitment campaign, of which the poster shown opposite is the most famous memorial, aimed to raise 100,000 volunteers in a month. In fact, it raised 500,000. How did the poster appeal to people's patriotism?

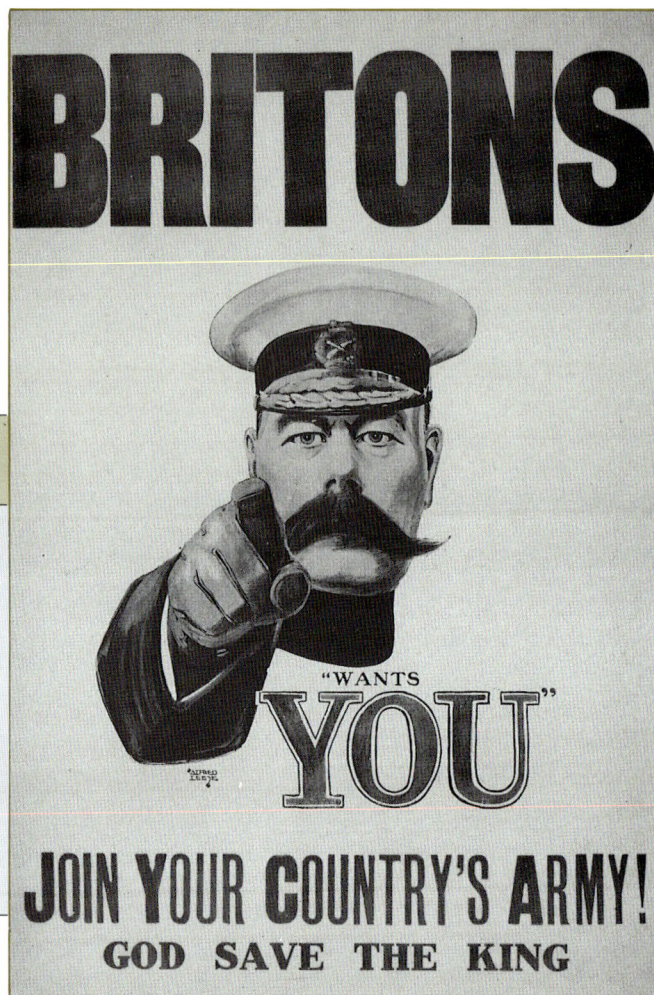

BRITONS "WANTS YOU" JOIN YOUR COUNTRY'S ARMY! GOD SAVE THE KING

THINGS TO DO

1   Find a local war memorial which lists the names of those who died in the Great War. Try to find out from your library or museum what proportion of soldiers from your area were killed.
2   Copy the picture of the British infantryman on page 11 and label his equipment.
3   Find out what you can about the Battle of the Somme and explain why, despite British losses, it has been described as 'the muddy field grave of the German Army'.

CHECK YOUR UNDERSTANDING

Can you remember the meaning of the following words and phrases?

Attrition
Conscription
Blighty
No Man's Land
Western Front

CAN YOU REMEMBER ?

How many men were lost on the first day of the British attack on the Somme?
Near which river was the German attack on Paris halted in 1914?
What happened at Messines in 1917?
Where were tanks first successfully employed in attack?
Where on the Western Front did the British army first go on the offensive?

Nothing Else For It

One reason why the men continued to join up and fight was that they feared the alternatives. At first the British army relied on volunteers. Young men who stayed at home were scorned and labelled cowards. From January 1916 conscription obliged every able-bodied man between the ages of 18 and 41 (raised to 50 in 1918) to put himself forward for military service. Refusal meant prison. Once in uniform any act that looked like cowardice, such as hesitating to go into an attack, might mean the firing squad.

> After the bombardment he [the Brigadier] sent out an officer and 25 men as a feeling patrol. As the patrol reached the German wire there was a burst of machine gun and rifle fire. Only two men regained the trench . . . The Sergent Major said, 'It's murder, Sir.'
> 'Of course it's murder, you bloody fool', I agreed, 'but there's nothing else for it, is there?'
>
> (Robert Graves' autobiography, *Goodbye To All That*, 1929)

The picture of French troops at Verdun below gives an idea of what it was like under fire.

Q

What did Graves mean by 'there's nothing else for it'?

Strategy

From late 1915 to the end of the war the British army was commanded by Field Marshal Sir Douglas Haig. No wartime figure is more controversial. He led the war of attrition, pounding away at the enemy lines at enormous cost in men and munitions, confident in the belief that in the end he would win through. The strategy did bring eventual victory, but it was also responsible for the terrible casualties. Was there really any alternative?

> Generalship is the most arduous and exacting of all human activities. It is a zero-sum game: win or lose. There is no in-between. What is not a victory is a defeat . . . Douglas Haig fulfilled the most important criterion of generalship. He won. The scale of his victories was the greatest in British military history. His countrymen have never forgiven him.
>
> (From British historian J. M. Bourne, *Britain and the Great War*, 1989)

IN THE TRENCHES

The trenches, in which millions of men spent months of their lives and which have become the Great War's most enduring symbol, were originally intended only as a temporary measure. Men were ordered to dig them to provide short-term shelter from enemy artillery and machine gun fire. Only later, when advance was impossible, did they become semi-permanent dwellings. Nevertheless, although by 1917 the Germans had accepted that an immediate breakthrough was unlikely and had withdrawn many men behind the specially prepared positions of the Hindenburg Line, General Haig refused to believe that trenches were anything but a provisional resting point before the advance was resumed. As a result, British living conditions were often worse than those of the men opposite them, sometimes as little as 50 metres away.

The two or three front-line trenches were generally about 2 metres deep, 0.5 metres wide at the bottom and 1 metre wide at the top. The front was raised with a parapet of earth or sandbags and protected by rolls of barbed wire. By standing on a firestep cut into the side, soldiers could see over the top. To avoid being hit by sniper fire, periscopes were sometimes used for observation. Narrow communication trenches zig-zagged back to support and reserve trenches in the rear. At intervals along the line there were dug-outs for the officers and supplies, and machine gun posts protected with concrete or, more commonly, sandbags. In wet weather the trenches soon filled with water. In the summer they became unbearably hot, dusty and smelly.

Trenches had no proper lavatory or washing facilities, and drinking water had to be brought to the front in cans. The soldiers did not go hungry, but they found the endless round of tinned food, jam, bread and dry biscuits was very tedious and led to serious constipation. That, together with feet so swollen after days in wet boots ('trench foot') that sometimes they required amputation, dysentery, lice, boils, flu and depressive mental exhaustion (known as 'shell-shock'), meant that the front-line troops were rarely in good shape for combat.

Boredom was another problem, for only a small fraction of a soldier's time was spent actually fighting. Most of his waking hours were taken up with inspections, the occasional patrol, meals, repairing trenches, caring for weapons, or just sitting about idly chatting and smoking. Enemy mining might be detected by placing a bucket of water in the ground and watching its surface for ripples caused by underground shock waves. When an offensive was launched, the men were not only unfit after taking no proper exercise for days, but weighed down by masses of equipment. This included a rifle, bayonet, steel helmet, grenades, ammunition, gas mask, water bottle, emergency food ('iron rations'), a small stove and fuel, wire cutters and a shovel. The whole lot weighed over 30 kilograms, making it even less likely that a man going 'over the top' would reach the enemy in a fit state to fight.

The artist Paul Nash's view of a front line soldier. Why do you think he entitled it simply Existence? *Can you suggest a title of your own?*

The scars of the pock-marked front lines have remained over the French countryside long after the fighting ceased. Note how close the lines are to each other.

IN THE TRENCHES

Machine gun fire and plentiful barbed wire barricades were generally quite sufficient to halt all but the most massive attacks. For much of the war the principal method of breaking down the enemy defences was the artillery barrage – the Battle of the Somme was preceded by a bombardment lasting eight days non-stop. This was supposed to smash trenches and cut barbed wire, although it rarely did so over a wide front. Other offensive weapons included poison gas (dependent upon the direction of the wind and therefore unpredictable) and, later, the tank. Tanks were first used on the Somme in 1916, but they were neither reliable enough nor properly used until the last year of the war.

Nothing Happens

Strangely, one of the major problems facing troops in the trenches was boredom. Attacks by one side or the other did not happen very often. Most of a soldier's life was spent cooped up in a tiny space carrying out routine tasks such as repairing the trench or cleaning weapons. This aspect of life at the front was described by the poet Wilfred Owen, who fought in France and was killed a week before the end of the war.

> The poignant misery of dawn begins to grow . . .
> We only know war lasts, rain soaks and clouds sag stormy.
> Dawn massing in the east her melancholy army
> Attacks once more in ranks on shivering ranks of grey,
> But nothing happens.
>
> (From the poem *Exposure*)

Q

Why was boredom a problem for troops in the trenches?

Too Good to be True

By early 1918 the importance of the tank as a weapon of attack had been recognized. At last a way had been found of getting safely over No Man's Land and through enemy barbed wire (see picture below). One tank driver remembered:

> It seemed almost too good to be true, this steady rumbling forward over marvellous going . . . Emerging out of the gloom a dark mass came steadily towards us – the German wire. It appeared absolutely impenetrable . . . but it squashed flat as we moved on, and remained flat.
>
> (Cited by Alan Lloyd in *War in the Trenches*, 1976)

An infantryman recalled:

> The Germans ran for their lives – couldn't make out what was firing at them . . . They didn't know anything at all about tanks, so the tank went on, knocked brick walls, houses down . . .'.
>
> (Cited by historian Lyn Macdonald in *1914–1918 Voices and Images of the Great War*, 1988)

Q

Why was the tank able to help break the stalemate on the Western Front?

The Machine Gun

The standard British machine gun was the water-cooled Vickers, capable of firing 450 rounds a minute (see picture below). In 1914 there were only two per infantry battalion, although the number in service increased rapidly, particularly after the formation of the Machine Gun Corps in October 1915. The 60 kilogram (three times the weight of the Vickers) German *Maschinengeweher 08* was similar to the Vickers in most other respects. But the Germans recognized the machine gun's importance before the British and had 12,500 in service in 1914. It was the *Maschinengeweher* which inflicted massive casualties on advancing Allied infantry.

A series of extended lines of British infantry . . . came on at a steady pace, as if expecting to find nothing alive in our front trenches . . . A few moments later, the rattle of machine gun and rifle fire broke from our whole line . . . Whole sections appeared to fall. All along the line, Englishmen could be seen throwing their arms into the air and collapsing, never to move again. Badly wounded rolled about in their agony, while other casualties crawled into shell holes for shelter.

(A German account of the Somme attack, 1916, cited by historian Alan Lloyd, *War in the Trenches*, 1976)

Q

Why do you think the British expected 'to find nothing alive in our front trenches'?

CHECK YOUR UNDERSTANDING

Can you remember the meaning of the following words and phrases?

Trench foot
Iron rations
Firestep
Parapet
Shell shock

THINGS TO DO

1 Visit the Tank Museum at Bovington in Dorset to see how the tank developed during the First World War.
2 List the advantages and disadvantages of using poison gas in an attack.
3 Write an imaginary account of a typical day in the life of a soldier in a front line trench.

CAN YOU REMEMBER ?

What was the name of the most popular British machine gun?
How deep was a typical trench?
What usually preceeded an infantry attack?
How was water brought up to the front lines?
What shape were communication trenches?

Of the almost 5 million men (nearly 25 per cent of the male population) who joined the British Army during the Great War, the great majority were concerned in some way with the war in France. But this should not obscure the fact that it was a *world* war, and the Western Front was only one of many regions where land fighting took place.

The slaughter on the Eastern Front, for example, where the British were not involved, was even worse than that in the west. Here a massive Russian Army of 7.5 million men, ill-trained and ill-equipped, tried in vain to resist the German advance. They lost 1.2 million casualties in the first five months of the war. Thereafter, although they had some success against the Austro-Hungarians further south, the Russians were gradually driven back until in 1917 the country collapsed into revolution and withdrew from the war. By this time over half the country's 12 million servicemen had been either killed or wounded.

There was less significant fighting in Africa, where the Germans were driven from their colonies in East Africa, South-West Africa, Togoland and the Cameroons, and in the Far East, where a handful of small German colonies were seized by Japan and the Allies. In 1917 some British divisions were sent to the Italian front. Their mission was to assist the Italians, who had entered the war on the Allied side in May 1915 and had just suffered a devastating defeat at the hands of the Austro-Hungarians at Caporetto. Over the next few months General Diaz reorganized the Italian army and was able to crush the Austro-Hungarians at Vittorio Veneto in the closing stages of the war.

The two other areas where British soldiers saw active service were Gallipoli, at the entrance to the Black Sea (see pages 18–19), and the Middle East. At the outbreak of war the empire of the Ottoman Turks, allied to the powers of the Dual Alliance, stretched from Constantinople in the west to Basra at the top of the Persian Gulf and Aqaba at the head of the Red Sea. The British sought to break up this empire with a three-pronged attack. An Anglo-Indian army landed in Iraq and gradually, after suffering several reverses, pushed its way up to Baghdad by 1918. The second front was commanded by General Allenby, who had been moved from the Western Front to Egypt early in 1917. He advanced through Gaza to Jerusalem and then on to Damascus, which he entered in October 1918. Meanwhile, an eccentric junior army officer named T.E. Lawrence had been helping the Arabian Arabs in their rebellion against their Turkish overlords. They cut the Medina-Damascus railway, took Aqaba in August 1917 and finally entered Damascus two months after Allenby.

A painting of 'C Beach', Suvla, in the Dardanelles. Men and munitions on the beach were often sitting targets for the guns in the hills above.

T.E. Lawrence, generally known as 'Lawrence of Arabia', the controversial British soldier who assisted the Arabian Arabs in their revolt against the Turks.

OTHER FRONTS

By 1915, when it was clear that the struggle on the Western Front was likely to drag on for much longer than expected, some of the more imaginative strategists (including the politicians Winston Churchill and Lloyd George) began to look around for a 'back door' into Germany. They hit on the idea of landing troops on the Gallipoli peninsula, on the western side of the Dardanelles, from where they hoped an advance could be made on Constantinople and Eastern Europe, to support the Russians on the Eastern Front. As it turned out, the troops from Britain, France and the Empire (mainly Australia and New Zealand) were pinned down by the Turks on the beaches where they landed and had to be taken off again eight and a half months later with the loss of about 250,000 men.

THINGS TO DO

1 Research the Eastern Front, drawing a map of it and marking in the major battles.
2 Find the present-day names of the German colonies of South-West Africa and East Africa.
3 Imagine you are an officer on the Western front. Write a letter to your MP arguing against establishing a front in south-east Europe.

CHECK YOUR UNDERSTANDING

Can you remember the meaning of the following words and phrase?

Colonies
'Westerners'
Ottoman Empire
Enlisted
ANZAC

A Logical Move

The idea of a Gallipoli landing was strongly opposed by 'Westerners', politicians and generals who believed any offensive not on the Western Front would just be a waste of men and materials. However, the plan seemed to make excellent strategic sense, as this cabinet minister explained:

> If we can take Gallipoli, [then] Rumania, Greece and probably Bulgaria will declare for us. [They] ... would throw an army of 1,500,000 onto the Austrian flank. This would not only relieve pressure on Russia but indirectly on France.

(Cited by Barry Bates in *The First World War*, 1984)

Australians charging enemy positions at Gallipoli, December 1915. Note the strange assortment of dress and lack of steel helmets.

Q

Why did the minister believe a Gallipoli landing would help the situation in France?

CAN YOU REMEMBER ?

When were British and French troops sent to the Italian Front? How many casualties did Russia suffer during the war? Name two leading advocates of the plan to land troops at Gallipoli. Which British general occupied Damascus?

Truly a world war: the British Imperial Camel Corps in the desert, 1917.

The ANZAC

Many of the men who fought at Gallipoli were from Australia, New Zealand (the Australian and New Zealand Army Corps, or ANZAC) and India. ANZAC Captain Guy Dawnay recalled the problems one group faced because the Royal Navy put them ashore a mile from where they were supposed to land:

> The landing place was a difficult one. A narrow, sandy beach backed by a very high intricate mass of hills ... How they got up fully armed and equipped over the rough scrub-clad hillside one can hardly imagine!

An anonymous Australian remembered the terrible fighting which followed. What makes this recollection so powerful?

> Well we reached the first trench, but not a Turk in it, they had cleared for their lives. The rifle fire became less but instead there was an awful tornado of shrapnel ... Fortunately I did not have to use my bayonet. I did not much relish the idea of sticking a man through ... [Later there began] tremendous rifle fire, from both sides – I had never imagined that rifle fire could make so fearful and everlasting a roar, it was wonderful in its awfulness.

> (Both extracts from contemporary accounts given in Malcolm Brown, *Imperial War Museum Book of the First World War*, 1991)

Q

Why do you think ANZAC troops were often bitter about what happened at Gallipoli?

19

A painting of the Battle of Jutland, 1916. Why do you think we get a better impression of this battle from paintings than from photographs taken at the time?

Before the war Britain had tried to maintain a 'Two-Power Standard', meaning the Royal Navy should be as large as the combined navies of any two other powers. However, in 1906 all previous calculations went by the board with the launching of HMS *Dreadnought*, an entirely new type of warship. Turbine-driven and with 12-inch guns mounted in turrets, the *Dreadnought* instantly made all other battleships obsolete. By 1914 Britain had 29 dreadnoughts (with 17 under construction) to face Germany's 13 and seven under construction. They also possessed 40 older battleships (compared with Germany's 22) and eight speedy battlecruisers to match Germany's five. The British also had about five times as many submarines as the Germans. Perhaps these figures suggest that Britain should have had an enormous advantage in naval warfare? But the reality was somewhat different.

The Navy's task during the war was to prevent supplies of food and raw materials reaching German ports from overseas, and to keep open Britain's worldwide trade routes by hunting down enemy raiders on the high seas and keeping the bulk of the German fleet bottled up in Wilhelmshaven. Their submarines were small, intended for coastal waters and harbour defence. However, helped by knowing the enemy's naval code, the navy managed its task quite well. 12,000 ships were intercepted on their way to German ports, less than 80 slipping through. By 1917 there were severe food and fuel shortages in Germany and factories producing weapons ran out of essential chemicals. During 1914 all German warships in non-European waters were either sunk or driven to port. However, the threat to Allied shipping posed by the expanding German submarine fleet was far harder to deal with. (See pages 22–23).

The British and German Grand Fleets were so valuable and so susceptible to damage from mines and torpedoes that both sides were afraid to risk full-scale combat. The Germans made small raids into the North Sea in 1914 and 1915, but only once did they bring the whole fleet of 99 vessels to sea. The resultant battle – Jutland – was one of the mightiest naval encounters of all time.

Having intercepted enemy radio signals, the British were ready for the German breakout. Admiral Beatty's force of battlecruisers and super-dreadnoughts sighted Admiral Hipper's scouting force on the afternoon of 31 May 1916 and immediately went into action. Hipper thereupon turned round to lure Beatty towards the main German fleet under Admiral Scheer. Suffering serious losses, Beatty met with Scheer and managed to draw him into the path of Admiral Jellicoe's principal British divisions. At 6.30 pm the two fleets met with a thunder of guns. Although the German shooting was more accurate than the British, whose ships were vulnerable to direct hits, Scheer eventually ran for home under the cover of darkness. After more confused fighting, by morning the Germans were safe back in harbour. Since he lost 11 ships to Jellicoe's 14, Scheer claimed victory. But his breakout had failed. The German fleet remained in port for the rest of the war.

Lord Beatty, who commanded the British battlecruisers at the Battle of Jutland. First making a name for himself as a shore commander, he was appointed commander-in-chief of the Grand Fleet later in the year.

WAR AT SEA

With their surface vessels bottled up in port, the Germans were quick to exploit the submarine (U-boat) as the best means of blockading Britain. By October 1917 they had 140 ocean-going U-boats. From 18 February to 1 September 1915 and from 1 February 1917 to the end of the war they attacked all shipping, Allied or neutral, in a war zone around the British Isles. By April 1917, when 423 ships were sunk, Britain was in danger of being cut off.

Then with the introduction of the convoy system (the major anti-submarine measure) and improved mines, depth charges and hydrophones (underwater listening devices) the stranglehold was broken. Nevertheless, by the end of the war German submarines had sunk over 11 million tonnes of Allied shipping, 8 million tonnes of which was British.

The *Lusitania*

On 7 May 1915, off the Irish coast, the German submarine *U20* fired two torpedoes at the liner *Lusitania* en route to Liverpool from the United States. The ship sank rapidly and 1198 people died, 128 of whom were neutral Americans. There was a huge public outcry. Below is the German justification for what happened. Was it significant that many Americans died?

> The 'Lusitania' was . . . armed with guns . . . Moreover it is well known . . . that she had large quantities of war material in her cargo. Her owners knew to what dangers the passengers were exposed. They alone bear all responsibility for what has happened.
>
> (An official German government announcement, cited in Barry Bates, *The First World War*, 1984)

Enter America

The USA declared war on Germany on 6 April 1917. The reasons for her action were complex. What explanation for the American decision is President Wilson offering here? Do you think the Americans had economic as well as moral objections to the policy of unrestricted submarine warfare?

> Vessels of every kind, whatever their flag, their cargo, their destination, their errand, have been ruthlessly sent to the bottom without warning or thought of help – the vessels of friendly neutrals, even hospital ships.
>
> (Cited in Barry Bates, *The First World War*)

Q

Why did the decision of the USA to enter the war on the Allied side force Germany to seek victory as swiftly as possible?

An artist's impression of the sinking of the Lusitania.

Submarine Attack

In his diary of 1917 Sub-Lieutenant Robert Goldrich of the convoy-escort sloop HMS *Poppy* remembered how hard it was to catch a submarine on the surface:

27 March: . . . Sighted her [a torpedoed merchant ship] at 10.30 am steering all over the shop. Steamed round her and found she had been torpedoed in No 2 hold just forward of the stokehold bulkhead. Sighted the crew in two life boats under sail and picked them up . . . While I was aft . . . 'Action' was sounded and I dived to the bridge to find a submarine panic on. I sighted the Fritz [German] 8,000 yards off high up out of the water but I did not see him soon enough . . . and did not get a round off. I was very sick about it 'cos she must have been watching us for some minutes.

(Quoted in Malcolm Brown, *Imperial War Museum Book of the First World War*, 1991)

U-boat captains were reluctant to use scarce torpedoes. They preferred to surface, give the crew of the merchant vessel time to abandon ship, then sink it with gunfire.

Q

Why was Goldrich disappointed not to catch the submarine on the surface?

CHECK YOUR UNDERSTANDING

Can you remember the meaning of the following words?

Hydrophones
U-boat
Convoys
Dreadnought
Blockade

THINGS TO DO

1   Draw and label a dreadnought battleship. What advantages did it have over ships of older design?
2   Research the Battle of Jutland. Write your own account of the conflict and explain whether you think it was a British or German victory.
3   Imagine you are sailing in a convoy – what measures would you take to guard against attack from U-boats?

CAN YOU REMEMBER ?

Which liner did U20 sink in 1915?
When did the United States enter the First World War?
Did the Royal Navy welcome the use of convoys?
Who commanded the German High Seas Fleet?
What were the tasks of the Royal Navy during the war?

WAR IN THE AIR

The highly manoeuvrable Fokker Triplane in the colours of the celebrated German pilot ace, the Red Baron.

The first heavier-than-air machine flew under its own power in 1903. When seven years later Louis Bleriot crossed the Channel in an aeroplane, the British military authorities realized, perhaps surprisingly, that the new machines were likely to play a significant part in any future conflict. The result was the formation of the Royal Flying Corps (RFC) in 1912. At the outbreak of war Britain was the only combatant country with a trained air force.

Fed by the needs of war, aircraft technology raced ahead. In 1914 the RFC's principal machine was the BE2, an unarmed reconnaissance biplane with a maximum speed of 120 kph. Over the next four years all sorts of developments took place. Most planes had two wings, but there were also fast monoplanes, such as the German Fokker, and ungainly-looking but highly manoeuverable triplanes, like the Sopwith 'Tripehound'. Aircraft were given more armour, bigger engines and

streamlining. Speeds rose to over 240 kph. They were used not just for guiding artillery fire and observation (in 1914 a sharp-eyed pilot helped Allied forces find a gap in the German advance), but for ground attack as well. Specialist long-range bombers appeared, some with two or more engines, carrying torpedoes or over 2000 kilograms of bombs. The Navy, too, began to use aircraft. The Royal Naval Air Service (combined with the RFC in 1918 to form the Royal Air Force – RAF) pioneered aircraft carriers and seaplanes, vital for anti-submarine work. By Armistice Day (11 November 1918) the RAF possessed 22,677 men in 188 squadrons.

The earliest planes had the crudest of weapons – hand-held rifles or even metal darts and bricks which could be dropped onto enemy aircraft from

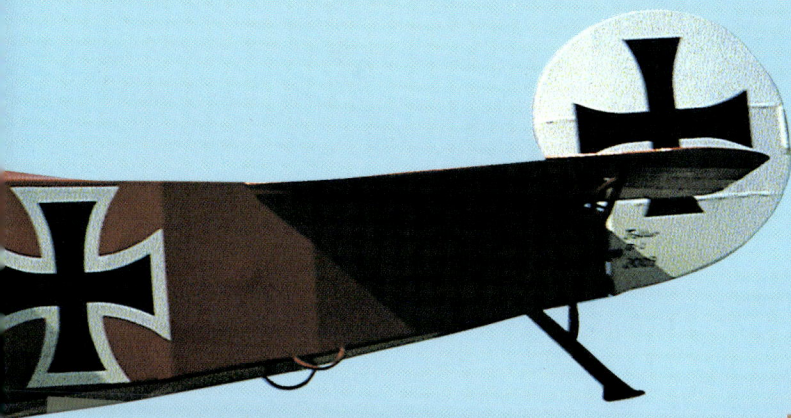

above. The machine gun was the obvious aircraft armament, although it was not easy to design a plane whose gun did not smash the propeller when fired. The British experimented with various ideas, like fitting the gun to the top wing, armour plating the propeller, placing the engine facing backwards ('pusher' planes) and swivel-mounted guns operated by a man seated behind the pilot. But it was the Germans who in 1915 came up with the ideal solution – an 'interrupter gear' (modified from a French design) allowing bullets to pass through the propeller without hitting it. Fitted with this device, the Fokker E-Type monoplane dominated the skies above the Western Front during 1915, downing over 1000 Allied machines.

Unlike the ground war, war in the air acquired a special romance. 'Dog fights' between groups of planes were a new, exciting form of warfare. The pilots were an educated élite. Non-uniformed, and unbelievably brave (the RAF refused to equip its pilots with parachutes), the successful ones, known as 'aces', became national heroes. But few pilots reached the status of Germany's 'Red Baron', Manfred von Richthofen (80 kills), Britain's Major Mick Mannock (73 kills) or Canada's Billy Bishop (72 kills). The life expectancy of an RFC pilot in the spring of 1917 was three months.

WAR IN THE AIR

Four things brought the horror of war from the front line to the people back home: shortages caused by blockade, conscription, terrible casualty lists – and bombing. Two types of machine were used for dropping bombs on enemy territory: airships filled with inflammable gas, and large aircraft. The Germans made 51 Zeppelin (the name of their famous airships) raids on Britain and 57 bomber raids, causing some 5000 casualties but doing little significant damage. The British replied with over 500 raids on German towns.

A Dog Fight

Captain Oscar Greg was shot down behind enemy lines while on a photography mission on 24 January 1917. His opponent was the famous Red Baron. What advantage did the German ace have by taking Greg by surprise?

At this moment I heard a machine-gun firing and saw several holes appear in the left wings. We were taken completely by surprise. I turned sharply to the right, banking steeply, hoping to get the enemy in front of me, but on completion of half a circle the enemy fired another burst from my right putting the engine out of action and hitting me on the right ankle. I continued in circles endeavouring to get a sight of the enemy but he succeeded in keeping below and behind my machine, making it impossible for either of us [the pilot and his observer] to fire at him while he continued to pour bullets into my machine.

(Greg's account is given in Malcolm Brown, *Imperial War Museum Book of the First World War*, 1991)

CHECK YOUR UNDERSTANDING

Can you remember the meaning of the following words and phrases?

Ace
Interrupter gear
Zeppelin
Dog fight
RAF
RFC

Q

Why was it important for the attacker to keep 'behind and below' his target?

The Zeppelin

What can you gather from this picture and these statistics about the strengths and weaknesses of a typical Zeppelin airship?

Range: 1000+ kms   *Bomb load:* 1000+ kgs
Speed: dependent on the wind   *Length:* 100+ m
Number built: 115   *Shot down:* 17   *Destroyed on landing:* 19   *Destroyed by accident:* 26

Q

Why do you think that one Zeppelin finished up over the Mediterranean after a raid on England?

THINGS TO DO

1   Research the topic of anti-aircraft devices (guns, searchlights etc) and say which were the most effective.
2   Draw a picture of a daylight bombing raid by either a plane or an airship.
3   Explain the ways in which aircraft altered the nature of warfare.
4   Imagine you are a fighter ace – describe a dog fight with your opponent.

CAN YOU REMEMBER ?

Why were 'pusher' planes used?
Did the Royal Flying Corps pilots wear uniforms?
How many planes did the Red Baron shoot down?
When was the Royal Air Force established?
Name one British triplane and one German monoplane used in the First World War.

Moral Outrage

Although they bombed Germany (one raid killed 26 women and 126 children), the British were infuriated by German raids. They regarded them as inhuman. What is this historian saying about the effect of bombing on British civilian morale?

The Germans were in many ways the perfect enemy. Their conduct throughout the war seemed almost designed to . . . galvanize public opinion in support of the war effort . . . British morale . . . [was] fuelled with moral outrage. Whenever it began to flag there was always another German 'atrocity' waiting round the corner . . . the sinking of the *Lusitania*, the use of poison gas, . . . the Zeppelin – and, later, the Gotha [a German heavy bomber] – bombing raids on civilian targets . . .

(J.M. Bourne, *Britain and the Great War*, 1989)

Q

What does the writer mean when he says that the effect of German bombing was similar to that of the sinking of the *Lusitania*?

Before the outbreak of the First World War Britain had been a bitterly divided nation. The two elections of 1910 saw the major parties, Conservative and Liberal, neck and neck. The mounting political strength and discontent of the working class manifested itself in waves of strikes and the rise of the Labour Party. There was serious trouble in Ireland, then part of the kingdom of Great Britain. The Liberal government's law giving the Irish home rule, due to come into force in 1914, threatened to plunge the country into civil war.

Then came the declaration of war, channelling anger and frustration away from internal disputes towards a common enemy – the Germans. Shops with German-sounding names were attacked. Even German breeds of dog, such as the dachshund, were frowned upon. The Royal Family changed its name from Saxe-Coburg-Gotha to Windsor. The newspapers (there was no TV or radio) filled with anti-German stories. The Irish problem was shelved, the number of strikes fell. In May 1915 prime minister Asquith invited members of all parties to join the Liberals in a coalition government in which politicians of every persuasion would be seen to be working together. The coalition was maintained by Lloyd George, who took over as prime minister in December 1916.

Gradually the life of every man, woman and child was affected by the war. Food and other goods ran short, and long queues formed outside shops. Eventually, beginning with sugar in December 1917, the government was obliged to order rationing, giving everyone the same allowance of certain scarce foods. It also introduced Summer Time to help farmers, allowed parks to be ploughed up for growing crops and limited the hours when pubs might open (and demanded watered-down beer). League football was cancelled. Prices and taxes rose. Buildings had to be blacked out to prevent their lights guiding enemy bombers.

The most dramatic changes were introduced through the Defence of the Realm Act (DORA), the Munitions Act, which forbade strikes in key industries, and 'Direction of Labour', a policy which empowered the government to move people from less important work to industries essential to the war effort. The very look and way of thinking of the nation was changed. It took some time for soldiers coming home on leave from the front to adjust to what had happened – to some of them wartime Britain was more like a foreign land.

Of course, not every one approved of what was done. Some left-wing politicians said the war was being fought for the capitalist classes rather than the British people as a whole. Price rises caused widespread resentment, especially when industrialists were seen to be making huge profits out of the war, and some strikes went ahead. Conscientious objectors (men who refused to fight) were sent to prison. But by and large the changes were accepted, and hardship was blamed more on the enemy than on the government at home.

This poster aimed to encourage men to join up. But in reality there was little chance of being killed by a bomb from a Zeppelin.

IT IS FAR BETTER TO FACE THE BULLETS THAN TO BE KILLED AT HOME BY A BOMB

JOIN THE ARMY AT ONCE & HELP TO STOP AN AIR RAID

GOD SAVE THE KING

Nurse Cavell was executed by the Germans for helping British troops escape from Belgium. Pictures such as this in **Le Petit Journal** *were used as propaganda at home.*

THE HOME FRONT

British patriotic and anti-German feelings arose partly of their own accord and partly as a result of deliberate government propaganda. Censorship made sure that no one wrote anything which might undermine public morale. Official statements played down defeats and lost no opportunity to denigrate the enemy as 'barbarians'. And, as we have seen (pages 26–7), every now and again – as in all wars – the enemy behaved in a manner which reinforced this image.

Recruitment

The government was amazed at the response to the appeal for volunteers in 1914 – 500,000 in August alone. All sorts of ways were used to attract young men into the services. What do you think the message was behind this recruitment poster?

WOMEN OF BRITAIN SAY – "GO!"

Q

Why have such posters been criticized as emotional blackmail?

CHECK YOUR UNDERSTANDING

Can you remember the meaning of the following words and phrases?

Conscientious objectors
Direction of labour
Blackout
Censorship
Rationing

CAN YOU REMEMBER ?

What was the new name of the Royal Family?
Who became prime minister in 1916?
What did DORA stand for?
Why was Edith Cavell shot?
How many men volunteered in August 1914?

THINGS TO DO

1   Devise your own army recruitment poster.
2   Imagine you are a soldier at home on leave (see adjacent picture). Write a letter to a friend in France in which you mention all the changes you have seen.
3   Write an imaginary newspaper article of December 1916 putting the best possible interpretation of the situation at the Western Front.
4   Find out from your local museum or library what was done in your area to help the war effort.

Censorship

Study the printed card below (right). It was given to troops for sending home from the front line. Why do you think they were not allowed to write more? (On the other side of the card it read: 'The address only to be written on this side. If anything else is added the postcard will be destroyed.')

Q

Troops behind the front were allowed to write longer letters. What sort of information do you think they were not allowed to give in them?

Propaganda

Edith Cavell was a British nurse shot by the Germans for helping Allied soldiers escape from German-occupied Belgium. How does the picture on page 29 use the incident to reflect badly on the Germans?

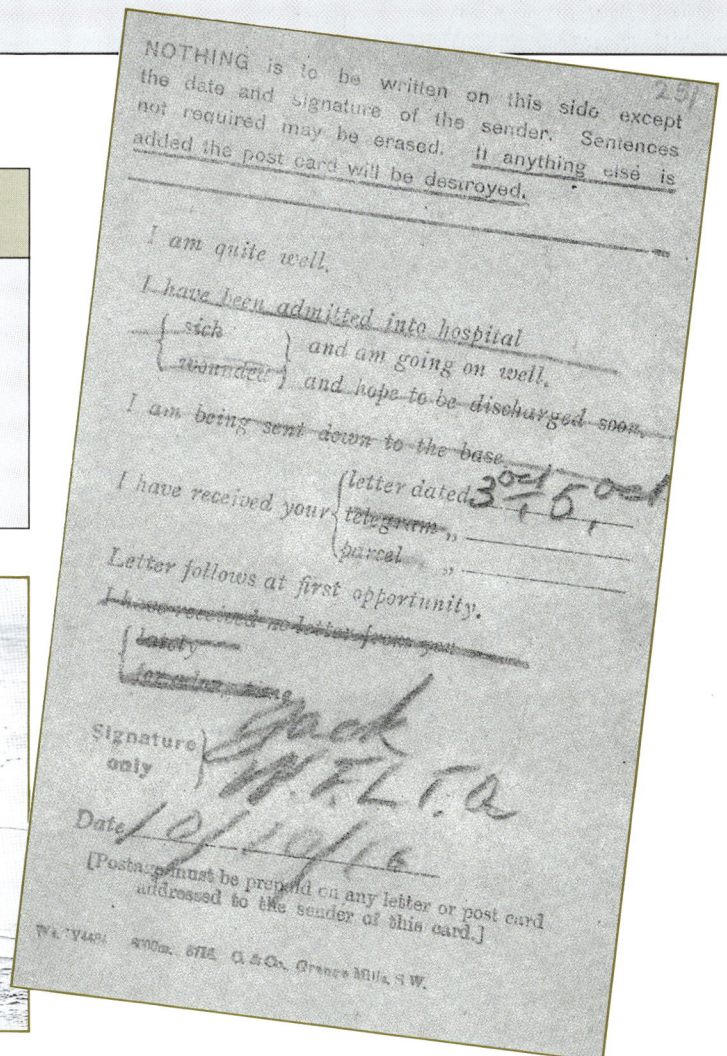

Children found it difficult to understand why adults were not allowed to tell them more about what was going on at the front. In a letter to his nephew, Robert Scott Macfie tried to explain the purpose of censorship:

I am not allowed to tell you where I am, because the General is afraid you might tell someone at school, and he might tell the German master, and the German master might telegraph to the Kaiser and tell him; and then, of course, the Kaiser would send an aeroplane to drop bombs on us.

(This letter is quoted in Malcolm Brown, *Imperial War Museum Book of the First World War*, 1991)

NOTHING is to be written on this side except the date and signature of the sender. Sentences not required may be erased. If anything else is added the post card will be destroyed.

I am quite well.

I have been admitted into hospital
{ sick
{ wounded } and am going on well.
} and hope to be discharged soon.

I am being sent down to the base.

I have received your { letter dated
{ telegram "
{ parcel "

Letter follows at first opportunity.

Signature only

Date

[Postage must be prepaid on any letter or post card addressed to the sender of this card.]

WOMEN AT WAR

In the years before the First World War women had been winning greater freedom. They gained the vote in local elections and became more active in politics. The spread of birth control released a growing number from the slavery of endless childbirth. Their dress became less restrictive. Gradually they were losing their status as second-class citizens. The war speeded up this process considerably.

The main reason why this happened was that with so many men away from home there was a serious shortage of labour. Anxious to 'do their bit' for the war effort, women eagerly took on jobs that had previously been done by men. This affected the middle and upper classes far more than the working classes, who were more accustomed to women working. The sight of thousands of wealthy women wearing trousers, cutting their hair short, soiling their hands with dirty work and mixing openly with men and women of other backgrounds at work was a terrible shock to many people. But they could not object – women's labour was indispensable. The consequences for women's position in society were enormous.

Some of the jobs taken by women – telephone operators, shop assistants, cleaners, nurses and secretaries – might have been expected. By 1917 over 650,000 worked in government offices. But other work broke new ground. Many women joined the Women's Royal Naval Service (Wrens) or the Women's Army Auxiliary Corps (Waacs), where they undertook all sorts of tasks except for actually fighting at the front. A quarter of a million women entered the Women's Land Army, doing the work of farm labourers who had joined the forces. Others became police or taxi drivers or engineering workers.

The most dangerous yet valuable work was done by the 820,000 women working in munitions factories, making the millions of bullets, shells, bombs and grenades needed at the front. They often worked in 12-hour shifts, seven days a week. The effect of handling chemicals sometimes ruined their health, making their hair fall out or turning their skin yellow. Despite government guarantees, women workers earned less than men (sometimes only half as much). Their presence was also objected to by male trade union leaders who thought women workers would bring down wage rates and put men out of work.

WOMEN'S LA[ND]

WANTED 5,000 EDUCATED WOMEN BET[WEEN]

Nevertheless, for many women war work and its wages brought a new sense of freedom, independence and importance. This was reflected in the way they dressed and behaved. For the first time they felt free to smoke, drive, and (for middle-class women) go where they wanted when they wanted. The increased emancipation of women was the greatest unforseen consequence of the war.

A poster calling on women to take over the work of agricultural workers who had gone to the front. The ability of women to work at least as efficiently and effectively as men came as something of a shock to many men.

WOMEN AT WAR

It was no coincidence that the Representation of the People Act of 1918 gave women (over the age of 30) a vote in parliamentary elections for the first time. A common expression at the time was that they had 'earned' the right to vote through their war work. It is more accurate to say that the war had shown women to be perfectly capable of doing just about everything that had previously been regarded as suitable only for men. (The adjacent picture shows a volunteer ambulance driver in France 1917). It was not they who had changed, but male attitudes.

Men and women alike

Like many men, J. L. Garvin, a newspaper editor, changed his attitude towards women as a result of the war. Why do you think this was?

> Time was when I thought that men alone maintained the State. Now I know that men alone never could have maintained it, and that henceforth the modern State must be dependent on men and women alike for the progressive strength and vitality of its whole organization.
>
> (The *Observer*, 1916)

From a middle-class family where women did not work, Joan Williams found the war gave her life a new purpose. Her job gave her freedom. She met people from all sorts of different backgrounds and for the first time felt she was doing something really worthwhile.

> I don't think any worker can have enjoyed their work more than I did . . . When I was on an interesting job it was nothing to leap out of bed at 5.15 on a frosty morning and I almost danced down . . . [the road] at the prospect of the day's work before me.
>
> (Joan Williams, *A Munition Worker's Career*, 1919)

Q

Why do you think that after the war women's status declined?

Women working in a factory making lenses. In many countries the ability to continue the war depended on the women's contribution.

Dining out

With their own money in their pockets and a greater sense of their own importance, women's behaviour began to alter, as the *Daily Mail* reported:

> The wartime business girl is to be seen any night dining out alone or with a friend in the ... restaurants of London. Formerly she would never have had her evening meal in town unless in the company of a man friend. But now with money and without men she is more and more beginning to dine out.

Munitions workers

Filling shells with the explosive TNT was dangerous work. It also had very unpleasant side-effects, as Caroline Rennles remembered,

> The Manager wanted us all to look like nurses, and he would say 'Look, tuck that hair under'. It was all bright ginger, all our front hair, and our faces were bright yellow. They used to call us 'canaries'.

(From Malcolm Brown, *Imperial War Museum Book of the First World War*, 1991)

Q

What class does the woman described above come from?

CHECK YOUR UNDERSTANDING

Can you remember the meaning of the following words and phrases?

Wrens
Munitions
Emancipation
Waacs

Q

Why were munitions workers known as 'canaries'?

CAN YOU REMEMBER ?

When were women over 30 given the vote in parliamentary elections? How many women worked in government offices in 1917? Which female organization took over the work of farm labourers now in the forces? How many days a week did women work in munitions factories? Were women paid the same wages as men?

THINGS TO DO

1   Imagine you are a female worker in a munitions factory in 1918. Write a letter to your MP saying why you think the war has proved that women should have the right to vote in parliamentary elections.
2   List the work done by women during the First World War.
3   Research women's dress between 1870 and 1925 and explain how it changed.

EXHIBITION
of WAR ECONOMY DRESS.
MUST · BE · SEEN · BY · EVERYONE
Grafton Galleries, Bond Street.
10 to 6. From 3rd to 31st August (Inclusive)

1818   1918

The National Standard Dress will be demonstrated by Mrs Allan Hawkey, The Inventor, who will Lecture Daily.

MANY OTHER ATTRACTIONS
Orchestra will play daily.
Admission 1/3d Inclusive of Tax.

Even dress fashions were affected by the war – it was unpatriotic to waste material!

THE FINAL YEAR

1917 had been yet another year of slaughter and stalemate on the Western Front. The huge British offensive near Ypres, begun with the attack at Messines Ridge, had finally slithered to a halt in the mud around the shattered village of Passchendaele. But elsewhere significant changes had taken place. The U-boat threat to Allied shipping had been defeated in the Battle of the Atlantic, and severe shortages in Germany as a result of the Royal Navy's blockade had slowly sapped the country's morale and ability to wage war. Moreover, German relief at Austria-Hungary's success against Italy and the collapse of Russia in November had hardly compensated for the entry of the USA into the war seven months before, though it would take the USA at least a year to mobilize her resources effectively. The German High Command had to move fast.

The result was the Ludendorff spring offensives. On 21 March 1918, after a 6000-gun bombardment, groups of German 'storm troops' rushed the Allied lines under cover of heavy fog and gas. In many places they broke through, pushing on to within range of Paris. But their casualties were enormous, and eventually the Allies were able to stop the advance. Ludendorff switched his attack to a British-held sector of the line near Lys. Once again his troops made large initial gains before grinding to a halt. Three further offensives, on the Aisne River, at Noyon-Montdidier and on the Marne, met similar fates. By July the German army had lost about half a million men and was totally exhausted. None of its strategic objectives had been met. The time was ripe for counter-attack.

A British tank, an early example of the weapon which was to revolutionize warfare around the world. They were first called **tanks** *– water tanks – in an effort to disguise their true purpose.*

A cartoon of Field Marshal Earl Haig, the controversial British supreme commander whose resolution cost thousands of lives but also probably helped bring about eventual Allied victory.

pressed on, pushing up towards the German frontier and liberating the Belgian coast.

Germany's allies began to drop out. The Bulgarians surrendered on 29 September, the Turks on 30 October and the Austro-Hungarians on 3 November. The German fleet mutinied. Riots and strikes erupted in German cities. The Kaiser abdicated. Finally, the new German government accepted the Allies' strict terms for an armistice, and at 11 am on 11 November 1918, the guns fell silent.

Marshal Foch, the French general who was given the awesome task of directing the final Allied assault on the German lines in 1918.

Now under the supreme command of Marshal Foch, the Allied assault began on the Marne on 18 July. Backed by hundreds of tanks and aircraft, a largely French force smashed through the German lines and advanced 8 kilometres on the first day. On 8 August Foch launched an even bigger attack near Amiens. By nightfall the Allies had progressed 17 kilometres, taking thousands of prisoners and many guns. In some places, for the first time in the war, the enemy had turned and fled. It was the 'black day of the German army' and the beginning of the end of the war. The final offensives began on 27 September. The French and Americans broke through in the south, the British and other Allies in the north. On 5 October the Hindenburg defensive line was breached. The next day the Germans called for an armistice – an end to hostilities. The Allies

THE FINAL YEAR

History is concerned as much with why things turned out as they did as with what actually happened. If one looks simply at the numbers of men on either side, Allied victory in the First World War might appear inevitable: 22 million servicemen from Germany, Austria-Hungary and Turkey faced 40 million mustered by the British Empire, France, Italy, Russia and the USA. But it was not as simple as that. Russian and American troops were never active at the same time. Although driven back, the German army was still intact at the end of the war and Germany was not invaded. The eventual Allied victory probably owed as much to the success of the blockade and the consequent turmoil in Germany as to any event on the battlefield.

Victory in the field

J. M. Bourne suggests that the eventual German surrender was forced by Allied victory in the field. What do you think he means by his first two sentences?

By the end of July 1918 Germany had lost the war. The Allies, however, had still to win it. The precondition for victory was the defeat of the German Army in the field.

(J. M. Bourne, *Britain and the Great War*)

Q

Why did the static war of October 1914 – March 1918 turn so suddenly into one of movement?

THINGS TO DO

1   Imagine you are a citizen of Berlin in the summer of 1918. Comment on the situation at home and the news from the front.
2   Draw a map of the Western Front showing the front lines in (a) September 1914 (b) December 1917 and (c) November 1918.
3   Research Field Marshal Haig and list his strengths and weaknesses as a commander.

German prisoners of war being brought to England, 1917. In some ways these men were the lucky ones – the picture on page 39 shows some of those on the winning side: gas victims, Estaire, April 1918. The men have all been blinded.

Endless horror

This comment by a member of the German government in October 1918 testifies to the effectiveness of the Allied blockade. How does it show the extent to which German morale had declined?

> We have no meat, potatoes cannot be delivered because we are short of 4000 trucks a day. Fat is unobtainable. The shortage is so great it is a mystery to me what the people of Berlin live on. The workers say 'Better a horrible end than an endless horror'.
>
> (Cited in Barry Bates, *The First World War*)

Q

Why was there a shortage of trucks in Germany?

Who was responsible?

Check the comment on Haig on page 11 and compare these two statements by living British historians.

> Foch's successful push [of 1918] led to the recovery of almost all of occupied France and part of Belgium before the Armistice. His achievements were widely acknowledged by the Allied governments as well as by his own country.
>
> (Anthony Bruce, *An Illustrated Companion to the First World War*)

> Lloyd George attributed this triumph of British arms [the victories during the autumn of 1918] to the guiding 'strategic genius' of Marshal Foch. He was wrong. The principal achievement was Haig's.
>
> (J. M. Bourne, *Britain and the Great War*)

Q

After the slaughter of 1915–1917, why do you think contemporaries were reluctant to recognise Haig's achievements of 1918?

CAN YOU REMEMBER ?

When did the Ludendorff spring offensives begin?
When was Armistice Day?
Who was given overall Allied command in 1918?
Did the Allies ever invade Germany?
What was breached on 5 October 1918?

CHECK YOUR UNDERSTANDING

Can you remember the meaning of the following words and phrases?

Armistice
Storm troops
Offensive
Counter-attack
The Battle of the Atlantic

THE LEGACY OF WAR

The ending of the war brought universal relief and, in the Allied countries at least, a tremendous outburst of rejoicing. Men and women wept with delight. They danced in the streets, paraded, sang and held parties to celebrate peace after almost four-and-a-half years of unprecedented misery. But the festivities did not last long. As soon became apparent, victory brought as many problems as it solved.

A ferocious epidemic of 'flu was sweeping Europe, carrying off millions weakened by poor diet and hardship. Virtually every family in Britain had lost at least one man. Countless thousands of ex-soldiers carried scars, mental as well as physical, for the rest of their wrecked lives. The politicians were faced with overwhelming tasks. The British economy, dislocated and damaged by the war, had somehow to be put on its feet again. The huge army had to be brought home, disbanded and jobs found for the men. At the same time, a permanent peace settlement had to be arranged. One that would ensure that never again would Europe have to face such a terrible war.

President Wilson of the USA put forward 14 points for a fairer world. Including such measures as allowing peoples previously within the Austro-Hungarian and Turkish Empires to form their own countries ('self-determination') and establishing a League of Nations to maintain world peace and justice, it was an idealistic yet unrealistic plan. The French, and to a lesser extent the British, wanted revenge on Germany. They blamed her for all that had happened. There were calls of 'Hang the Kaiser!' and 'Squeezing Germany till the pips squeak!' A fairer world was hardly likely to emerge from such an atmosphere, and it did not.

The Treaty of Versailles, which Germany was forced to sign in 1919, imposed terribly harsh terms on the defeated nation. She was made to admit that her aggression had started the war and ordered to pay £6,600,000,000 reparations (compensation) for the damage she had caused. Her colonies and many parts of Europe inhabited by German-speaking peoples were taken from her. She was excluded from the new League of Nations and allowed no air force and only a tiny army and navy. Her allies were subjected to similarly harsh treaties. A patchwork of freshly-created small countries (such as Czechoslovakia, Yugoslavia and a separate Austria and Hungary) dotted the map of Europe, at the heart of which lay a depressed, humiliated Germany. Although at the time many believed this was a sure recipe for enduring peace and security, history was soon to prove them dreadfully mistaken. The conflict of 1914–1918 had certainly been a Great War, but it had not been, as was popularly thought at the time, 'the war to end all wars'.

The enormous war cemeteries of north-western Europe remain a horrifying memorial to the millions from all over the world who died in the Great War. This one is at Tyne Cot in Flanders.

(Opposite) *Signing the Versailles Treaty, 1919. Although intended to offer a just and lasting settlement, the treaty was so unfair that even at the time people were dismissing it as a mere 'ceasefire'.*

THE LEGACY OF WAR

Britain did not, as many had hoped it would, 'return to normal' with the onset of peace. Indeed, after so many dramatic changes no one was quite sure what 'normal' was any more. Many of the most able men of their generation had volunteered in the early years of the war. Now almost all of them were gone for good, resting in the long lines of simple graves that checkered the French countryside. The economy went into recession. A new wave of strikes began. Women were depressed to find the new status they had enjoyed during the war eroded when the men returned. What on earth had it all been for?

The voice of the poet

Rupert Brooke, who died in 1915, wrote these lines in December 1914:

> If I should die, think only this of me:
> There is some corner of a foreign field
> That is for ever England . . .

Siegfried Sassoon, who fought on the Western Front and survived the war, wrote this in 1929:

> Do you remember the dark months you held the sector at Mametz –
> The nights you watched and wired and dug and piled sandbags on the parapets?
> Do you remember the rats; and the stench
> Of corpses rotting in front of the front line trench . . . ?

Q

How are the moods of these two poems different? Do you think the difference in the dates when they were written is significant?

THINGS TO DO

1   Research the Treaty of Versailles and draw on a map of Europe the territories which were taken away from Germany.

2   Imagine you are a British MP in 1919. Write a speech calling for Germany and her allies not to be treated too harshly.

3   Imagine you are a German soldier who had fought on the Western Front. What is your reaction to the terms of the Treaty of Versailles?

4   From these figures work out which country had the highest casualty rate in the First World War:

COUNTRY	SIZE OF FORCES	CASUALTIES
Austria-Hungary	7.8 million	4.8 million
British Empire	9.5 " "	3.0 " "
France	8.4 " "	5.6 " "
Germany	11.0 " "	6.0 " "
Russia	12.0 " "	6.6 " "

Vengeance!

The humiliation of Versailles deeply wounded Germany's pride. Why does this German newspaper article call for 'vengeance'?

> Today in . . . Versailles the disgraceful Treaty is being signed. Do not forget it! The German people will with unceasing labour press forward to reconquer the place among nations to which it is entitled. Then will come vengeance for the shame of 1919.
>
> (Deutsche Zeiting, 1919)

Q

Why did the writer think the Versailles treaty 'disgraceful'?

Refugees fleeing from an advancing army. As in any war, from 1914–18 the suffering of innocent civilians was particularly distressing.

Blame

The causes of the First World War were long-drawn-out and complex. However, in the 1919 Treaty of Versailles the victors made it quite clear where they believed the blame lay:

> **The Allied . . . Governments affirm and Germany accepts responsibility . . . for causing the loss and damage to which the Allied and Associated Governments and their nationals have been subjected as a consequence of the war imposed upon them by the aggression of Germany and her allies.**
>
> **(Clause 231, Treaty of Versailles)**

Q

Do you think such a statement accurate? What do you think most Germans thought of it?

The peacemakers, 1919: (left to right) prime minister Clemenceau of France, president Wilson of the USA and British prime minister Lloyd George.

CAN YOU REMEMBER ?

How much was Germany asked to pay in reparations after the First World War?
What was the name of the treaty imposed on Germany in 1919?
Who suggested the formation of a League of Nations?

CHECK YOUR UNDERSTANDING

Can you remember the meaning of the following words and phrases?

Reparations
Self-determination
Terms
Vengeance

Why was the Women's Land Army formed?

Why were trenches first dug?

What was the British Expeditionary Force?

Why was a coalition government formed in Britain?

Which British commander is most closely associated with the policy of attrition?

Why did the USA enter the war?

What happened in Russia in 1917 to take the country out of the war?

How did the war affect British women?

Why was conscription introduced in Britain?

How might the Treaty of Versailles be criticized?

What was life like in the trenches?

TIME CHART

1871	German Empire proclaimed
1879	Austro-German Dual Alliance
1892	Franco-Russian military agreement
1904	Anglo-French entente
1905	Schlieffen Plan settled
1906	HMS *Dreadnought* launched
1907	Anglo-Russian entente
1914	
June	Archduke Franz Ferdinand assassinated in Bosnia
July	Austria-Hungary declares war on Serbia
August	Germany declares war on Russia
	Germany invades Belgium
	Britain at war with Germany (4th)
	Troops of the British Expeditionary Force in France
	Defence of the Realm Act
	British troops fighting at Mons
	Germans defeat Russians at Tannenberg
	Naval battle in North Sea
September	German advance halted
	Germans defeat Russians at Masurian Lakes
October	Trench warfare begins on Western Front
Oct–Nov	1st battle of Ypres
	Turkey joins Germany and Austro-Hungary
November	Britain begins blockade of Germany
December	British naval victory near Falkland Isles
	German fleet bombards British coast
1915	
January	1st Zeppelin raid on Britain
	Naval battle in North Sea
Feb–Sep	Unrestricted U-boat warfare
Apr–May	2nd Battle of Ypres
April	Allied landings at Gallipoli
	Easter rising against British in Ireland
May	Coalition government in Britain
	Italy joins Allies
September	Allied offensives at Loos and Champagne

December	Haig created British Commander-in-Chief
1916	
January	Conscription introduced in Britain
February	Germans begin attack on French positions at Verdun
May–Jun	Battle of Jutland
June	Russians begin offensive on Eastern Front
July–Nov	Battle of the Somme
December	Lloyd George becomes Prime Minister
1917	
January	Unrestricted U-boat warfare (to end of war)
February	Germans start to withdraw behind Hindenburg Line
March	1st revolution in Russia
April	United States declares war on Germany
	British offensive at Arras begins
	Mutinies in French army
May	Convoys first used
June	British capture Messines Ridge
	First American troops in France
July–Nov	3rd Battle of Ypres
October	Austro-Hungarians defeat Italians at Caporetto
November	Communist revolution in Russia
	Tanks successful at Cambrai
December	Rationing introduced in Britain
1918	
March	Russia signs Treaty of Brest-Litovsk with Germany
	German offensives on Western Front begin
	Foch created Allied Commander-in-Chief on Western front
July	Allied advance begins
August	'Black day of the Germany Army' (8th)
October	British pierce Hindenburg Line
November	Austria-Hungary signs armistice
	Armistice on Western Front (11th)
1919	
June	Treaty of Versailles signed

Western Front 1914–1918

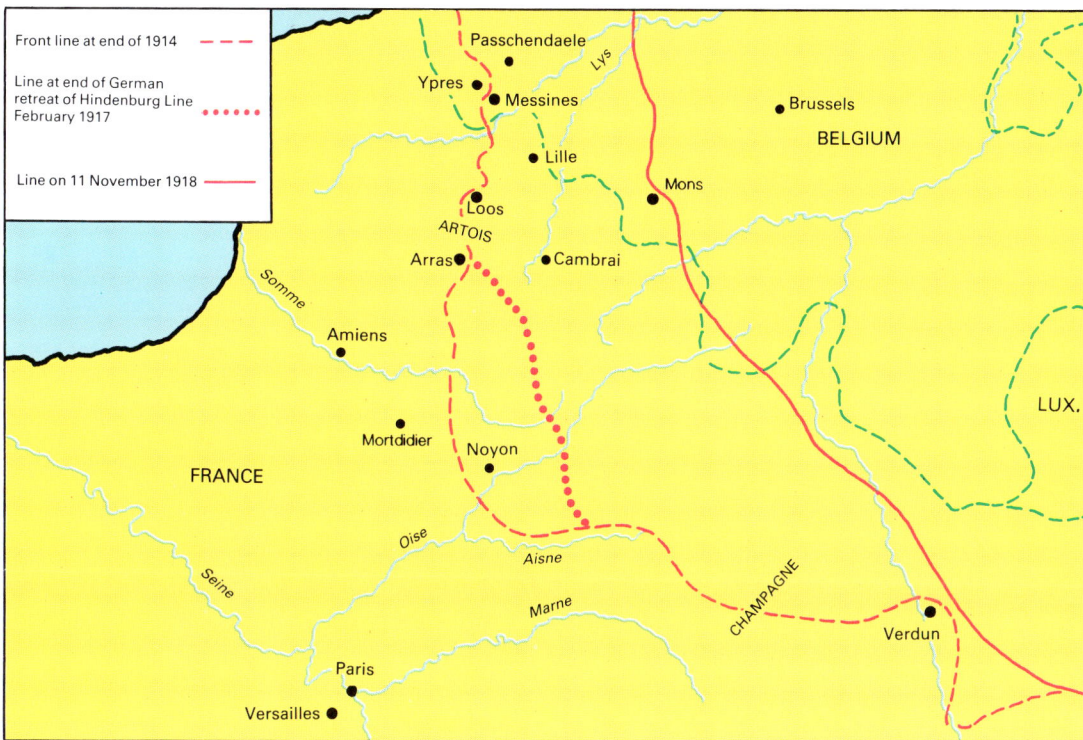

Front line at end of 1914	– – –
Line at end of German retreat of Hindenburg Line February 1917	• • • • •
Line on 11 November 1918	———

Passchendaele
Ypres
Messines
Lys
Brussels
BELGIUM
Lille
Mons
Loos
ARTOIS
Arras
Cambrai
Somme
Amiens
LUX.
Mortdidier
Noyon
FRANCE
Oise
Aisne
Seine
CHAMPAGNE
Marne
Verdun
Paris
Versailles

Campaigns in Europe 1914–1918

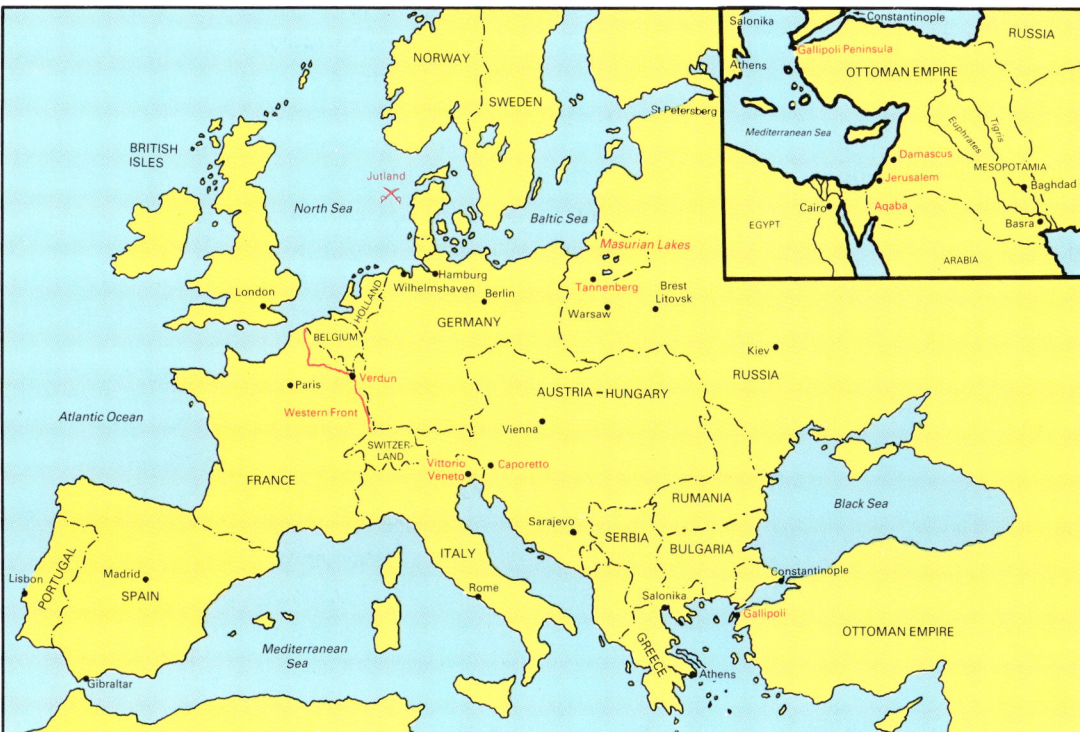

NORWAY
SWEDEN
St Petersberg
BRITISH ISLES
Jutland
North Sea
Baltic Sea
London
Hamburg
Wilhelmshaven
Berlin
Masurian Lakes
HOLLAND
BELGIUM
GERMANY
Tannenberg
Warsaw
Brest Litovsk
Verdun
Kiev
Paris
RUSSIA
Western Front
AUSTRIA – HUNGARY
Atlantic Ocean
SWITZER-LAND
Vittorio Veneto
Caporetto
Vienna
FRANCE
RUMANIA
Sarajevo
SERBIA
Black Sea
PORTUGAL
ITALY
BULGARIA
Constantinople
Lisbon
Madrid
SPAIN
Rome
Salonika
Gallipoli
OTTOMAN EMPIRE
Gibraltar
Mediterranean Sea
GREECE
Athens

Salonika
Constantinople
RUSSIA
Athens
Gallipoli Peninsula
OTTOMAN EMPIRE
Mediterranean Sea
Euphrates
Tigris
Damascus
MESOPOTAMIA
Jerusalem
Baghdad
EGYPT
Cairo
Aqaba
Basra
ARABIA

GLOSSARY

alliance An agreement between countries to fight together

ally A country fighting alongside another

Allies, the Britain, France, Russia, Italy, the USA and the other countries fighting with them

armistice Ceasefire

artillery Heavy guns

attrition The strategy of defeating the enemy by wearing them down

Balkans The land between the Black Sea and the Adriatic

battalion An army unit of about 850 men

bayonet A knife which fits on the end of a rifle

Blighty The British soldiers' slang word for home

blockade Cutting a country or town off from outside supplies

bombardment A large artillery attack

bunker A strong underground shelter

casualties Those killed or wounded

censorship A policy of cutting out unacceptable words or pictures

coalition Government of more than one party

colony A country's overseas possession

conscription Compulsory military service

convoy Many ships or vehicles travelling together

dog-fight A battle between fighter aircraft

dreadnought A class of fast, heavily armoured battleships

dug-out A shelter dug into the earth

dynasty A ruling family

Eastern Front The battle lines between Russia, Germany and Austria-Hungary

emancipation Setting free

empire Many lands under one government

entente Agreement

firestep The ledge on the forward side of a trench

front The battle line nearest the enemy

grenade A hand-held bomb

Home Front A country in wartime where there is no actual fighting

ideology Set of beliefs

infantry Soldiers who fight on foot

iron rations Basic food

isolated Cut off

morale The mood of a country or force

mortar A short-range bomb thrower

munitions Ammunition

nationalism Strong feeling of approval for one's country

neutral Not taking sides

No Man's Land The land between opposing front lines

offensive Large-scale attack

Ottoman Empire The Turkish Empire

parapet The low wall on the side of a trench nearest the enemy

propaganda Information designed to deceive or affect morale

province Part of a country or empire

recruit Take someone into the armed forces

reparations Compensation

round A single bullet or shell

sector Part of the battle line

shell A large exploding bullet, usually fired by artillery

shell-shock Depression caused by the strain of fighting for a long time

sniper A sharp-shooter

strategy Overall campaign plans

TNT Trinitrotoluene, a high explosive

treaty An agreement between countries

U-boat German submarine

ultimatum A final demand

Western Front The battle line to the west of Germany, running through France and Belgium

Zeppelin German airship

FINDING OUT MORE

For younger readers

Bates, Barry, *The First World War*, Blackwell, 1984

Evans, David, *The Great War 1914–18*, Edward Arnold, 1981

Mair, Craig, *Britain at War*, John Murray, 1982

Ross, Stewart, *Lloyd George and the First World War*, Wayland, 1987; *Origins of the First World War*, Wayland, 1988; *War in the Trenches*, Wayland, 1990; (ed) *The First World War*, Wayland, 1989.

Two very interesting videos are available from the Imperial War Museum: *The Battle of the Somme* and *War Women of Britain*.

For older readers

Brown, Malcolm, *The Imperial Museum Book of the First World War*, 1991

Bruce, Anthony, *An Illustrated Companion to the First World War*, Michael Joseph, 1989

Gilbert, Martin, *First World War Atlas*, Weidenfeld and Nicholson, 1970

Lloyd, Alan, *War in the Trenches*, Grenada, 1976

Macdonald, Lynn (ed), *1914–1918 Voices and Images of the Great War*, Michael Joseph, 1988

Marwick, Arthur, *The Deluge*, Penguin, 1967

Remarque, E. M., *All Quiet on the Western Front*, Putnam, 1929

Sassoon, Seigfried, *Memoirs of an Infantry Officer*, Faber, 1930

Stevenson, John, *British Society 1914–45*, Penguin, 1982

Taylor, A. J. P., *The First World War*, Penguin, 1976

Places to visit

As well as your local museum, you will find material on the First World War at the Imperial War Museum (London and Duxford), the RAF Museum (Hendon), the Bovington Tank Museum (Dorset), the National Army Museum (London) and the National Maritime Museum (Greenwich). At several sites in France the lines and dug-outs of the Western Front can still be seen. A visit to the numerous war cemeteries in France and Belgium brings home the scale of the slaughter of 1914–18 more effectively than any book.

Acknowledgements

The Author and Publishers would like to thank the following for their kind permission to reproduce illustrations: the Imperial War Museum for pages 1, 9, 10, 13, 16, 17, 20, 25 (bottom), 33, 39, 41; the Mary Evans Picture Library for pages 5, 11 (left), 21, 29, 37 (top and bottom); the Hulton Deutsch Collection for pages 11 (right), 22, 23, 26, 34 (bottom), 38, 43 (bottom); *After the Battle* magazine for page 12; Aviation Photographics International for page 25; e.t. archive for page 28; the Tank Museum, Bovington Camp for page 36; Peter Newark's Military Pictures for page 40; and Dave Davis (illustrator) for the four maps on pages 4, 6 and 45.

The cover illustration shows *Over the Top* by John Nash, and is reproduced by kind permission of e.t. archive.

Thanks go to the *How It Was* series editors for advice and editorial input: Madeline Jones, Jessica Saraga and Michael Rawcliffe.

INDEX

Numbers in **bold type** refer to illustrations.